Evasion Therapy

poems by

Charlie D'Eve

Finishing Line Press
Georgetown, Kentucky

Evasion Therapy

Publisher: Leah Huete de Maines
Editor: Christen Kincaid
Cover art: Charlie d'Eve
Author photo: Andy Costello
Cover Design: Elizabeth Maines McCleavy

Order online: www.finishinglinepress.com
also available on amazon.com

Author inquiries and mail orders:
Finishing Line Press
PO Box 1626
Georgetown, Kentucky 40324
USA

I would like to thank my dear friends Cai and Lindsey for reminding me that life is a delicate balance of inconvenience and absurdity, and therefore it should not be taken too seriously. I would also like to thank my father for always encouraging any and all of my endeavors, no matter how fruitful the outcome, and my mother for providing the nurturance I needed at my lowest of lows.

You would think / You would have a life plan

In the hospital / The floral wallpaper will love you

Your mother, her arms around her purposeless tummy

You, in the corner evacuated

Moaning on the purple plush couch

Ma   ma   ma

There she goes / Turning on the instructional

video Light blue bulging off her hand

A woman with a chiffon blouse saying

Welcome

Through the tv box

When my momma come up te me

& say here I am loving and ready

for your loving

I pull out her long cow jaw

I take away her aspic skin &

There it goes in my toy chest all goopy jellyfish

My hands slap slap congratulations

My baby mouth aroused

If I could I bet

I bet I woulda pulled her damn eye out

Here I am having made my

movement as wide as

my shame can go

I never want to talk to

my sad clown face in the mirror

or the jawless woman

I end up with both under my feet

Finally, it's my voice that says

    Congratulations says

You owe me

You're in my house

What I mean to say is

I was a child

I danced naked round the four cornered kitchen

til

Adults clapping into their red sauce

Sissy threw me off the bunk bed and my head became a

Watermelon falls out the window and makes a

Real mean splash

I'm a lil bonkers see

Friend high fiving me, "Definitely"

Remember how well I slept with

the man outside my house watching me?

Wasn't a man but a

Very angry fowl cawing

Come come here little buddy

The only way was to

put a pen in my nose and spend the day

in plastic wrap

When Austin ate his ants I ate the Sports section

The only person who could tell me I was dying was

The doctor down the street

He pulls my neighbor's tooth out of

        My other neighbor's bicep

        on a Monday

The col-de-saq kids we

All laugh when we see him next   Lil Gappy

Pops was on a business call when

I ran over the family dog my

Tinsley basket popped off

The doctor brought us into his hole where

I threw up gingerbread cookies into chunks

It was after that we nicknamed him

        Dr. Blood

She had a lot of blood to give

When we called in sick to school

We watched Looney Tunes

Mom wasn't looking when I

tied strings around my teeth

then

pushed the door closed

There are   things I   don't forgive and   let's be
honest here

It is usually the things I am most often doing

& usually related to what is in my hands

Mother thought I tried to

                Get her gut with dull scissors

That's when she saw my art project

lying on the floor

That's the night the glue spilled as she tryta

M a t r I x   away

What I mean is some of us

                Start our life

                assuming malice

I put on my headphones before I even

get out the door

You can tell a lot from the bottom of someone's feet

                Such as, look at me!

Look at the purple splotch that waits to fall off me

Look into my mouth

I am trying very hard to tell you another time

Cai was sitting on the edge of the cliff when

Cai said she had to get her glasses back

From someone else's home

She left as they

Glistened atop her head

Not the fact that she's dead but

the fact that she hasn't come back

to my house to

return my Avett Brothers shirt

It's always the same when someone asks

How did it happen

Avert   er   t

hm

no

It happened like this:

A girl walks into a bar and says / Where's the nearest pool

A girl walks into a kiddie pool and says

This'll work

There's control in telling someone

Their fly is down

I got the text at the park I used to do acid in

It happened yesterday

        Why didn't anyone call

When someone is dead I forget about them

        no

        When someone is dead I l

        ook at m

        y body &

        Gross

When I look at the skin on my chest

        I know

I'll lay flat on my bed &

        grab at my hip bone making sure it's

        still with me

Cai died slowly

Carry me won't you?

We'll play

Light as a feather stiff as a board

Light as a feather

As long as my body is

        So litterl

        So smol

        Almost all gone in that cold air

Here I go wondering when to be

Satisfied with how my body

    Box is always too big too many

When my friend tells me I should "   "

I don't think the world of him

After all don't you know

If you were meant to breathe that much you'd

probably be on Earth

Okay—A red cup soiree

Elegance was triple sec,

A game of chess I thought I'd figured out

We soaked the board with maple syrup once I'd won

Back then, my eyeliner was all wings

& she with her half filled green tea
frap Listening to 3Oh!3 on the 5

Dying my hair in my parent's bathroom

out of town on Christmas

Still mad about the pink stain next to their brand new sinks

We had mouths that always mouthed

N o n o n o

Where did that go?

We had a whole vocabulary of things we hadn't tried yet but

Already loved

Last time she dropped me out of her car

French fry filled burrito in hands

I said I think I love that man

She said *dead if you don't try*

Dead if I don't

The first time it happened she

Saw a reef underneath

Something calling to her

Something telling her it's time to come home

When we got to the

When we got to the funeral home

her mother asked what size said

I can't remember what size

        I looked in each box

        Goldilocks

Wrapped my hands around the sides,

        Dippd my head in & pointed to three

        She said

        None of those

        Are the

        Same

The story of the dead girl goes like this:

She started as a child & then she

   grew

  whole silver panes around her body

Tin girl

They thought she was

    Ra, God of the sun

    & put her on the roof of her family

    home for all to see

  No one could look into her panels when

   the sky was too red

& yet

monsoon season

  when the fish cracked their heads

  down Mt. Lemmon

in her, they saw their own reflection

All she could see was

  the circumference of her hips,

the ratio of thighs to

waist

  Always looking down at her

If I put a whole other body in my body yes I'd be best

If I puta whole Other skin

     Oh shit that's me!

       I make myself central daily, these days

       she aint with me but

Dr. Blood still mails me

There is a point in the day when my body kicks out Then

     I can sneaks

I can run and   I can run

Dog coughs up black cat hair

Did you know?

       Tyra Banks thinks that I should eat a steak

     There are whole sections of the internet dedicated to

Unique

Small

Art

Related

Items

Summer again, and I don't have a single hole in my body

I haven't closed up

I do have a mom (alive)

I don't want to master the worm in your bedroom

Come to mine,
                    I'll make us pancakes

His hands were sweating on a Tommy Bahama

            In the back of an old Chevy, chalky yellow &

            Windy with one liners

Make a banana pancake

When he fell asleep to Survivor

I   sharpied the bottom of his car

                    I

                    threw up in the elevator on the way back up

I left the party without a shirt on

Dropped my body in a pothole on Main st.

When I got to my house

            My father with his legs crossed running round

            screaming

Chicken

Pka Pka

7/11 parking lot with

     a man I didn't know shouting

     "Get the fuck out of here!"

          pirouetting on his bike, mean eye hanging out
          right on me

          Rouge as a baboon ass

A (alive) girl followed after asked

if I was afraid

     said   she was afraid

     How can that angry wheelie man just bark

Doberman, desert heat

& then the guy came back and made

     himself bigger in my skin

     Not bigger than my skin, or so my skin

couldn't Just to see how far my lig'ments

          Could stretch under the weight of him

When you stop looking for the ground girl you

        end up in a Walmart parking lot in the middle of

        Amarillo, Texas with a man around your gut

        You

        end up in a

            army base with families you don't know

            watching Ghostbusters, eaten by
mosquitos

I made friends with an eleven-year-old cello with a dead
                    mom

I learned

when a woman plays a song on spoons,

        I don't throw a dollar. I buy a diet coke

        I become smaller than most town's potholes

        My head always stays wet & above ground.

        The tabby cats

        claw

at my car stickers all night. Sleeping in the

        trunk with a tiny fan in my hand

Once I walk outside me I

        am walking right back in

        pulling closed the blue door

        with my cold bony toes

Friend asks if I'd do me

Nah

        Too many miles

Just kick me with

the damn golden boot

With enough semen in me I can translate   my   own
me   correctly

At a party once I fell asleep

on a trampoline

When I woke up:

        Man with the weird beard bouncing above me

        Trying to crack the egg

Tell me the story of the woman unfolding

    her honesty

    out of her hands

A finger curling to make a tactile O

Fourth fing straightening a lanky I

        Ring falls off

    The only way I know how to relate to

    My friend who whos sad crawls down the street

    pet on a leash

is through the pictures I shadow man who sits in my bed

        that I

    cry off to

I am not a good friend (was)

I won't pass back the Pringles

& then

        They're gone

That's what I've been trying to say

Here are the holes you can put your hate into:

between your fingers pointing

right back at you

I broke my rearview mirror when I finally

Got back to school

Dear Therapist #7:

I don't want to look like a cockroach when I give a farewell

I don't want to shit my pants

I cried when I put my brand new white shoe on

& kicked at the belly fats too late sayin

Get this damn guy off of me

How can the body be in the kitchen

pouring a Jack n coke & then

tucked up under a cabinet with feet hanging in the air?

Little Charlie coming out of me

In thousands of small sighs daily

I watched a man cry for a dollar when

The other man said cry for my dollar

I watched a woman shake

That's when the ambulance finally came

When did we stop looking for the water?

Was it us who forced the spigot to

dry out?

I am trying to look at the picture of my lucky in greater detail:

There is the house

There is the me

Up the steps and turning into

Holding the important papers that I cannot lose

The good news is that: I have a place to run to

I have a door that locks

I say cheers to a body that wakes up every morning

My face never turns off

There are kinds of anger you can't avoid being placed on
you

Even the ones you put on you

        The dog ran out & the girl (me) shouted after it

        Dear, dear

        Where are you dear

        From the window I watched her yowl

        At least the dog came back

I have figured how to earn my hinges

& Now look:

I can say that is done. I can say

        I am mobile watch me play hanky panky

in the backyard while the lights are out

I will pull all of my clothes off

If you are naked, yes, you run fast

If I were given the chance, I'd

    get on the plane to find the

    rose to put inside me

    It's speckled little reds

    hold myself and my notta million dollars saying

    farewell, farewell

I don't know where the rose is but I know it's not in my house

Not watching the oven plate dry on the rack

Not looking in the fridge for its keys

If you put it in your stomach you will hear the click
& I know I want it

At the waist of a dug out or in a bloated trash can

a tooth will hurdle over a lip

and hand me my vase

    My handsome weighty vase

    The light will turn on and there – look

There go the rouge petals

Charlie d'Eve is a writer, jeweler, and tattoo artist nestled in Portland, Oregon. She has an MFA in creative writing from the University of Arizona, and is the recipient of the Margaret Sterling Award, the Poetry Center Award, and The Academy of American Poets Award at Portland State University. You can find a multitude of her artistic endeavors at *@charliedeve.tattoo* on Instagram.

www.ingramcontent.com/pod-product-compliance
Lightning Source LLC
Chambersburg PA
CBHW022058080426
42734CB00009B/1409